The Jungle Cat Hybrid and Chausie Manual

by
Chuck Cunningham
Black Panther Publishing

Black Panther Publishing
Sarasota, Florida
www.BlackPantherPublishing.com

The Jungle Cat Hybrid and
Chausie Manual

Publishing History
Printed October 2002

Printed in the United States of America

Table of Contents

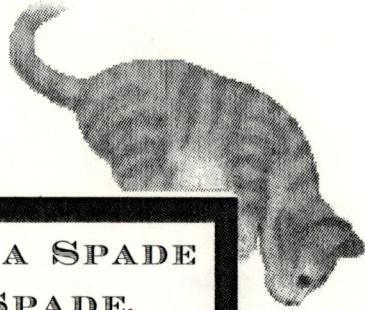

> CALL A SPADE
> A SPADE.
> DECLAWING
> IS
> AN
> AMPUTATION!

Chapter One

What Is a Jungle Cat?

"Mongo the Bondsman"
Our Pure Jungle Cat Posing for the
Action/Thriller Novel
The Jade Claw
A Story About a Man and His
Beloved Jungle Cat
Available at: BlackPantherPublishing.com

JUST A THOUGHT

BREEDERS WHO SHIP CATS VIA
THE AIRLINES
SHOULD FIRST BE MADE TO
CRAWL INTO A SMALL
CONTAINER AND THEN RIDE
ACROSS THE COUNTRY IN THE

DARK

BELLY OF AN AIRCRAFT, NEXT TO
ALL TYPES OF TERRIFIED
ANIMALS, JUST TO SEE WHAT
IT FEELS LIKE.

Chapter One

What Is a Jungle Cat?

The Jungle Cat has a rich history dating back thousands of years. They are believed to have been owned by pharaohs in ancient Egypt. Some stories have it that they were trained by the Egyptians to take down fowl. They are capable of vertical leaps of over ten feet. It was once believed to be one of the ancestors of the domestic cat but recent DNA testing has refuted the claim.

The Jungle Cat (felis chaus) is a medium sized wild cat. The males generally weigh between 25 and 30 pounds. The females are somewhat smaller weighing between 15 and 25 pounds. Their geographic location is NE Africa to Thailand and Vietnam, Sri Lanka. They are not an endangered species and no accurate population count has been made however; several resources put the total count over one hundred thousand. Jungle Cats are a protected species in some areas but the protection is not strictly enforced.

They are extremely adaptable and are born survivors. I like to refer to them as "the coyotes of the cat world." They are often found in and around human settlements and are great chicken thieves. In Kashmir, they were reported to occupy "nearly every old building about Srinagar," and recently, in southern India, a breeding pair was found occupying an old building in an urban area near coconut palm plantations.

Unlike the name implies, they prefer river bottoms and swampy areas to jungles. Their main diet consists of rodents, birds, and small game. They have been seen in the wild taking down small pigs.

They are strong swimmers, and will dive to catch fish, or to escape when chased by man or dog. They are extremely intelligent. One cat in India, observed hiding in a bush while stalking a group of gray jungle fowl, appeared to make deliberate clockwise movements of its head, rustling leaves and attracting the curiosity of the birds.

Other names given the Jungle Cat are Nile Cat, Reed Cat, and Swamp Cat. These names are much more fitting. When people find out we own Jungle Cats one of the first questions they ask is "What kind of jungle cat is it?" When most hear the name "Jungle Cat" they immediately associate it with something more along the lines of a leopard or black panther. Although a beautiful cat he is very different from his wild cousins.

The Jungle Cat has long legs and a slender build. The fur is generally sandy brown, reddish, or grey, and is unpatterned except for stripes on the legs. Although more rare some of them will have melanistic (black) coats and silver tip coats, which are black coats with lighter fur tips. Jungle cats have black ear tufts. The tail is relatively short, generally coming only down to the hocks. Their coat color is similar to that of a mountain lion. They carry the agouti ticking gene and this is responsible for the coat color. The agouti ticking gene causes the individual hairs to have bands of light and heavy pigmentation. It allows for full pigmentation when the hair starts to grow, then slows down the synthesis of pigment for a while, and then turns it on for a while. As the hair approaches its normal length and stops growing, pigment synthesis stops. The result is a hair shaft that has dense pigment at the tip, then a band of yellow to orange, then a band of dense pigment, fading to yellow to orange at the root. Usually the jungle cat kittens will be born with a grayish and spotted coat. As the cat matures, the hair grows the tips become lighter and give the cat its permanent or adult coat. This can be seen in a lot of the hybridized offspring. I have had 50% wild cubs born with very definite spotting on their coats and as they approached adulthood the ticking gene kicked in and they lost almost all of the spotting leaving only barely recognizable "ghost" spots.

They reach sexual maturity between eleven and eighteen months and have between one and six offspring with the average being three. The number of offspring in the wild can vary with the amount of available food. Their gestation period is about the same as a domestic cat which is about sixty to sixty-five days. The male is very protective of the cubs and they have been seen traveling and hunting as a family unit.

I am often asked whether Jungle Cats make good pets and why I don't sell them. My answer to the first part of that question is NO. When I purchased my first Jungle Cat the breeder swore up and down what a great pet he would make and they would get along fine in the house. Well, it didn't take me too long to find out the truth. They are extremely active and can get up on anything and love to get into everything. They love to chew and shred things like pillows and couch cushions. I did not buy a wild cat just to cage it so I put up with it. I ended up buying replacement furniture at the Salvation Army thrift store about every three to four months. You can have nothing out on the table or counters. They love the highest place around and to try to keep them off counter tops, etc., is an exercise in futility. Forget carpeting. That all had to come out and be replaced with tile.

What else, let's see... oh yes, he took out two different TV sets by jumping up on them and when he kicked against them to leap off, down they came. I have one on the wall now that is bolted to a stand. He also was extremely bonded to me and very territorial. He would snarl at anyone who came over and stayed for any length of time. I bought another jungle cat from another breeder and the result was the same. Both of them are in the house at least four nights a week now and I do love and enjoy both of them; however, my house is stripped to bare bones. Anything I wish to keep is in a locked cabinet or a closet. For any wild cat you also need a very large outside cage with logs, tree limbs, etc. The roof needs to be covered to prevent escape. They need fresh air and a place to be able to run and exercise. Their moods can change in a heartbeat from being very loving to giving you the "back off" look and you had better back off. I have learned every move of my cats and have the utmost respect for them. If you have children you are putting your child's safety in jeopardy by having any wild cat around. Even the best of cats will defend themselves if someone steps on or falls on them accidently. A Jungle Cat is a medium sized cat but they have very powerful jaws. I have seen them pulverize turkey drumsticks in minutes.

Chapter Two

What Is a Jungle Cat Hybrid?

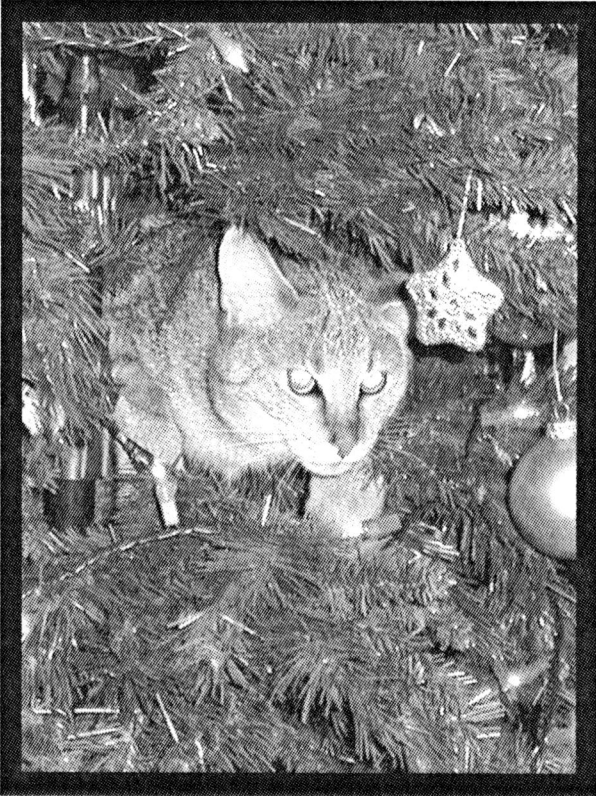

"Kamala" a Jungle Cat
Hybrid, Female.
Bred by Mandala Exotic Cats,
Sarasota, Florida

THERE IS NO
SUBSTITUTE FOR
A MOTHER CAT'S
CARE AND NURTURING
BOTTLE FEEDING
ROBS THE CUBS OF
THIS IMPORTANT PHASE
OF
DEVELOPMENT.

Chapter Two

What Is a Jungle Cat Hybrid?

A Jungle Cat Hybrid is any cat that is the result of mating a Jungle Cat with any type of domestic cat. Breeders use many different types of cats depending on the desired outcome. Some use the Bengal if they wish the offspring to have spots. Some will use the larger breeds like the Maine Coon if they wish more size. Some use black cats only to try to produce a panther type cat. The list goes on and on. Here at Mandala Exotic Cats one of our main thrusts has been size so we have only used larger cats and also choose to use the "polydactyl" (extra-toed) gene as polydactyls tend to carry thicker, heavier frames. Chausies are Jungle Cat Hybrids also but are bred with only one goal in mind and that is to produce a cat resembling the Jungle Cat. This will be discussed in the following chapter. That seems to be a point of confusion as I get many inquiries asking me "What is the difference between a Jungle Cat Hybrid and a Chausie?" For the time being just try to remember that a Chausie is a Jungle Cat Hybrid and most things in this book will pertain to both. The differences will be noted where necessary. And an explanation will follow shortly. So, be patient, we will get there.

Concerning wild hybrids you will often hear breeders use the terms F1, F2, F3 and so on to designate the type of hybrid they are referring to. The "F" stands for "filial" generation and the number designation is the number of generations that the cat is removed or "down the line" from its wild parentage. To make this a lot simpler to understand let's look at some examples. If a pure Jungle Cat is bred or crossed (this is the common term used by breeders) with a domestic the offspring are one generation removed from its wild ancestry. Therefore the offspring "F" designation is "F1" and would have fifty percent wild blood and fifty percent domestic blood. Now if one of the F1, fifty percent wild blood, offspring is mated to a domestic again the resultant offspring would be designated "F2" wild hybrids and have only twenty-five percent wild blood.

Now, suppose we mated a "F2"(twenty-five percent wild blood) again to a domestic the offspring would be "F3's" and contain only twelve and one half percent wild blood. See the chart below. The "X" stands for "mated to" or "crossed with."

Jungle Cat X domestic = F1 offspring, 50% wild blood

F1 hybrid X domestic   =F2 offspring, 25% wild blood

F2 hybrid X domestic   =F3 offspring, 12 1/2% wild blood

This can go on *ad infinitum*. To confuse you further, if for example an F1 is mated to an F5 the lowest designation is always used in determining the "F" designation of the offspring. See examples below.

F1 hybrid X F5 hybrid = F2 offspring, approximately 28% wild blood (you do the math)

F2 hybrid X F4 hybrid = F3 offspring, approximately 16% wild blood

I tried to go over this in detail and make it as simple as possible. It's basically grade school math. Understanding the "F" or "filial" designation is a very valuable tool when searching for a Jungle Cat Hybrid or a Chausie. Anyone that breeds wild hybrids will know exactly what you are talking about and which type of cat you prefer when you mention the "F" grouping. Later on we will discuss size, temperament, etc., of the various filial generations to better equip you in your quest, if it's just for information you seek or you are looking into adopting a cub.

I should mention although female hybrids are capable of reproducing, most, if not all, F1 males are sterile. F2 males are occasionally fertile but are not reliable at all. Some F3 males can reproduce but it is still not a sure bet. Some can be fertile for a short time and then become sterile later on.

DID YOU KNOW THAT IN JUST
SEVEN YEARS,
ONE UNSPAYED CAT AND HER OFF-
SPRING CAN PRODUCE OVER
450,000 CATS?

Chapter Three

What Is a Chausie?

"Fool's Gold"
A
Beautiful Chausie

BUYING AN ANIMAL
OVER THE
INTERNET AND
HAVING IT FLOWN
TO YOU
IS LIKE BUYING A
"PIG IN A POKE"

Chapter Three

What Is a Chausie?

A Chausie is a Jungle Cat Hybrid that is bred specifically to look like the pure Jungle Cat. The name was derived from the scientific name for the Jungle Cat—Felis Chaus. The goal is to retain the looks but to introduce domestic blood to make the cat a pet that would fit into any home environment. For all practical purposes the desired outcome would be a cat that resembles a Jungle Cat with a domestic temperament. There are many breeders hard at work trying to produce such a cat. They are trying to get the breed to be recognized by several different cat associations and granted "show" status. It is a lot of work and a lot of red tape to work through to get a new breed recognized. First of all to be able to show a cat at a sanctioned show the cat must be at least an F4 or have only about 6 1/4% wild blood. One of the problems encountered in this pursuit is that the domestics that would fill the bill as suitable out crosses are generally smaller or average sized domestics. One of the first things that one loses in out crossing to a smaller cat is size. After a Jungle Cat's line is out crossed four times to get to an F4 I cannot imagine a cat much larger than some of the existing domestic breeds that are already out there. There is no "size" requirement in the "Chausie standard."

I have answered a ton of e-mails from people inquiring about Jungle Cat Hybrids and Chausies and almost always one of the first questions is "How big will it get?" Almost everyone wants a large animal. For that reason I have chosen to stay with breeding Jungle Cat Hybrids. I keep only big cats in my line and am more interested in producing a large, feral/wild looking cat with a great temperament than I am in producing a smaller one that looks like a miniature Jungle Cat. Both are great looking cats. But to each their own and I in no way am belittling the efforts and all of the hard work that is going on presently with those who wish to show their cats. It is only a matter of personal preference.

Those interested may view a copy of the acceptable Chausie Standard at The International Cat Association's web site at http://www.tica.org.

Chapter Four

Is a Chausie or Jungle Cat Hybrid Right for Me?

Two Beautiful
Wild Hybrid
Cubs

Seen on a Breeder's
Website:

I love my animals
and
treat them as I
would
my own children.
Will ship anywhere.

Chapter Four

Is a Chausie or Jungle Cat Hybrid Right for Me?

I believe it's always a good idea to make an informed decision before purchasing any pet. Below are some of the things that should be considered and looked at in detail before attempting to purchase a wild hybrid. I have fielded a ton of questions concerning the behavior of hybrids and will try to answer most of the more common ones here.

1.) Do they get along with other pets?

They seem to do well if bought at a young age and introduced to the other pets slowly. Usually it's more of a question of how the other animals will accept the hybrid rather than the other way around. They are very playful and active.

This can pose a problem if you have an older, more laid back cat that would rather sleep than play. As kittens they can be a real bother to these "older guys." On the whole, they seem to be able to adapt to whatever situation they are introduced into as long as the introduction is done when they are young. I have noticed some problems when once the hybrid is established in a household and then you try to introduce another cat. Sometimes their "territorial" instincts will kick in and the adjustment to a new family member may take some time.

2.) Do they get along with children?

This is a tough question because it depends a lot on how well behaved your children are. If your children respect animals and are able to interact without pulling on it's ears or tail they should be fine. You have to remember though, a lot of my F1 hybrids have gotten to over 25 pounds and that is a large cat. Any cat when startled or stepped on accidently will attempt to defend itself. They are not aggressive but I would monitor my child's behavior and make sure the interaction between pet and child is one of respect as with any other animal for that matter.

The F1's can also get wound up and play a little too aggressively. If a child starts running around and lets the hybrid chase it they can get carried away at times. The best thing in this instance is to give the cat some "time out" and let it mellow out for a few minutes. Never yell or physically punish the cat. This NEVER does any good. To be honest, I have never had any reports of any children being bitten aggressively. F1's a lot of the time, to get your attention will bite on your arm say if they wish to be petted. This can be a little unnerving if one does not know what the cat is doing or becomes afraid. F2's , if bred properly, have about the same qualities as any domestic. Face it, almost every kid gets scratched by a cat once in their lifetime. Usually it's unintentional and they probably will get scratched by a hybrid somewhere down the line but usually from playing.

3.) I work all day and am gone from my home, is this OK?

First of all I don't believe any animal should be expected to be left alone for extended periods of time. Animals are like humans. They are social creatures and need interaction with humans or other pets. If you have another cat that is playful and the two can wear each other out and get along fine, then

I would say that it's OK to leave them alone for brief periods of time. If you do not, then I would never get one. If left alone they will act out by becoming destructive and sometimes stop using the litter box. They may even get aggressive and anti-social. I always suggest to people who do not already own a cat to go to the local pound and get the most active kitten they can find for a companion. That way your cub has a playmate and you have done a good deed by rescuing an animal from possible euthanasia.

4. How big of an area do they need?

They seem to do fine in an average sized house or apartment as long as they have the run of the place. If you are thinking of keeping one in a separate room or out on the patio, then please don't get one. They do not liked being "cooped up" anymore then you would.

5. Are they destructive?

They are no more destructive than any other cat except a lot of them go through a teething phase much like a puppy would. Most of mine seem real fond of electrical cords for some reason but a little "bitter apple" spray available at all pet shops seems to cure this problem.

6. Are they expensive to keep and maintain?

The health care required is no more expensive than for any other cat. You will need routine shots, check ups, neutering/spaying fees , etc. They will eat more than a regular cat and therefore the feed bill will be a little higher but not outrageous. Diet and veterinary care are discussed in a later chapter.

7. What sacrifices need to be made?.

As mentioned earlier having plants are almost out of the question. If you are the type that has a lot of knick knacks, plates on display, etc. most of these will have to be put away if you intend to keep them intact. For the first year you will have to get used to a cat that is very active and "in your face" a lot. After a year or so they seem to mellow considerably.

Chapter Five

Selecting a Breeder

"Mongo" posing
again.

THE AIRLINES SIMPLY
DO NOT CARE ABOUT
ANIMALS AND HANDLE THEM
NO BETTER THAN A PIECE OF
LUGGAGE.
THEY ADAMANTLY OPPOSE
ANY NEW LEGISLATION
CONCERNING ANIMAL SAFETY.

Chapter Five

Selecting a Breeder

Important points to look for when selecting a breeder.

1.) How many different breeds does the breeder work with?

I have seen breeders that have servals, jungle cats, domestics, and the list goes on. They also sell Chausies and Jungle Cat Hybrids and claim to raise all of them "underfoot" and they are "all a part of the family." I have raised only hybrids for years and I have my hands full. There is no way anyone with multiple breeds can be expected to do a proper job and put in the necessary time to properly raise and socialize all of the different breeds they claim to work with.

2.) Does the breeder have a list of references?

Any breeder should readily be able to furnish you with a list of references. I have seen breeders advertise cats that are "capable" of getting very big. Well an Abyssinian is "capable" of getting very big but seldom does. If you are interested in size, beware, a lot of breeders have one or two cats that have gotten quite large and they usually have pics to prove it. But is that rare or is that the norm with the breeder? Face it, breeders are in the business to sell you a cat. Although almost all claim that their cubs or kittens are "part of the family" and this can be true in some cases, most still want to sell you a cat. The old adage is "Ask a man who owns one." Get the references and ask the owners a ton of questions. If you were looking into buying a car and you were talking to a Chevrolet salesman I am sure he would tell you nothing but good things about this and that type of Chevy. However, after consulting with seven or eight owners you may get a different point of view. The same goes for the cat trade. A lot of hybrid sales are handled over the internet where the buyer never lays eyes on the breeder and never even sees the cat until they pick it up at the airport so more or less as the farmer said "You are buying a pig in a poke." It behooves you to take your time and do your research well.

3.) Does the breeder ship animals?

I must say I am always amazed that breeders claim that they love their animals and treat them like children but do not hesitate to drop off a little kitten at eight or twelve weeks of age to be stowed away in the dark belly of loud aircraft and flown across the country alone. This is very traumatic to any animal regardless of breeder claims. I know of many owners that claim that their cat that they got from a breeder that was air shipped hid under the couch for days, heavily traumatized and terrified to come out. Presently the air lines claim that 99% of the animals arrive without incident. That is what they "claim" but are not required by law to keep records so I suspect that the percentage is quite higher. Even if it isn't, 1% loss is still way too high and odds I don't care to take. "Counter to Counter" shipping only means that instead of dropping the kitten or cub off in a cargo hangar it gets dropped off and picked up at the counter. Do not be fooled by this type of shipping. The cat still has to face the most harrowing part of the flight alone, scared, and will be traumatized. I do not and will never ship unescorted pets. Airlines will let a passenger take up to two kittens on board where it can travel next to the new parent and not next to a barking Doberman in a cargo bay. If the kitten is indeed a part of the family and treated like one of the children it would be the equivalent of taking an eight month old child and placing it in a cage with a bottle and some baby food and putting it through the same gauntlet. I doubt any sane parents would tolerate such a thing. There are many ways to get a pet to the owner. A lot of time two kittens will be going to the same area and one of the owners can fly or drive in and get both of them and split expenses. There are other possibilities also; it takes some effort on the breeder's part as well as the owner's but it can be done.

Another reason breeders like to ship animals is that they don't like you to see the condition the animal is raised in. It's very convenient to just feed the customer a big line, have the customer order the cat over the net, drop it off at the airport and you never have a chance to lay eyes on them or their facility. I personally know of one breeder on the East Coast, in a mid-Atlantic state that kept his cats with his whole family in a double wide mobile home. Due to lack of space the cats, jungle cat included, were kept in small wire cages. His cattery had experienced almost every type of disease known to the cat world at one time or another. Cats were sold out of his facility even while some of his animals tested positive for FIP! Now this guy was a "quick study", could talk a great line, but his "hands on" care was deplorable. So, "buyer beware," visit the facility, pick up your pet!

4.) Is the breeder prompt and courteous?

The breeder should be available to answer any and all questions regarding the sale and care of the cat. He or she should answer all inquiries either by phone or e-mail in a timely manner.

5.) Other things to look out for when selecting a breeder.

Cheaper is not always better. If the price looks too good to be true then it probably isn't a good deal after all. Beware of anyone advertising things such as "discount prices," etc. I would be leery of older kittens that are not sold yet. However some breeders do sell "retired breeders" and many of these are sold at lower than market prices and do make good pets. They have paid their dues and then some and deserve a good home.

Above all take your time. Impulse buying, especially where animals are concerned, can lead to disastrous results. Hybrids generally live 15 years so you are going to have the cat a long time so take your time in selecting one. It is a good idea to find a breeder you are comfortable with and get on a waiting list and wait for a cat that will be the closest there is to fulfilling your needs. I have had many people call or e-mail and ask if I have any cats available and if not immediately go to the next on the list. It's like they have to have one "now." The last available cat may not be the best cat. I have also had many just price shopping for the cheapest cat out there. Most hybrids raised properly are not cheap because the time and care it takes to raise them properly and maintain healthy breeding stock is not cheap. Most breeders that are any good "keep their day job." They are not getting rich overnight.

Also find out how many litters the breeder has per year.

If I have six litters per year then I am busy almost full time socializing and caring for them. Also ask how long their queens are rested between litters. A good rule of thumb is that a female should have no more than three litters in two years or one litter every eight months. Responsible breeders will use this time table. Queens should be retired after having four to five litters. That is enough kids for any woman to raise.

BOTTLE FEEDING OF
CUBS IS AN INHUMANE PRAC-
TICE AND HAS LITTLE, IF
ANYTHING, TO DO WITH HOW
WELL THE ANIMAL WILL BE
SOCIALIZED OR HOW WELL IT
WILL BOND TO HUMANS.
LEAVING THE CUBS WITH
MOM AND CONSTANT HAN-
DLING AND ATTENTION ARE
THE ANSWERS.

Chapter Six

Preparing for Your New Arrival

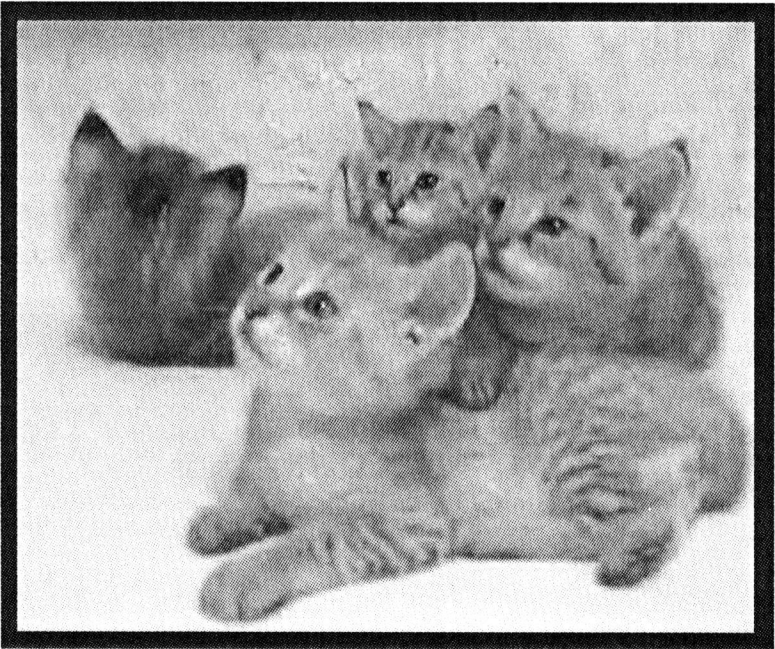

**Beautiful Cubs
at
Five Weeks Old**

WHEN YOUNG CUBS ARE PULLED FROM THE MOTHER AT 5-10 DAYS OF AGE TO BE BOTTLE FED THE MOTHER GRIEVES AND COMES BACK INTO HEAT BELIEVING THAT SHE LOST THE LITTER. THERE IS NO EXCUSE FOR ADHERING TO THIS PRACTICE.

Chapter Six

Preparing for Your New Arrival

So you have listened to all the good and bad and have decided that you would love to be the proud owner of a hybrid. You have found a breeder by now and need to get things ready on the home front. There are of course the normal things to get such as a litter box and litter, feed dishes, pet carrier, kitten chow, etc. Regular low litter boxes are good at first but if you get a hybrid from large parents you will have to move up to something bigger. I prefer to use the larger plastic, storage bins available at most discount stores. You should be able to find one that is about 24" long by 12" high by 16" wide for about five dollars. I generally put in about 25 pounds of litter and with the larger, deeper box the cat can scratch around without throwing litter all over the place.

As previously mentioned these guys are very smart and can learn to open cabinet doors and later on even pull drawers open. It's a good idea to get child-proof locks on cabinet doors that contain toxic substances especially like under the sink. A lot of plants are toxic to cats. After looking up all of the possible toxic plants I found so many I decided it was easier to just not have any. If you do have plants and they are safe you can count on them being destroyed in a short time after your kitten's arrival anyway. Christmas trees, unless you plan on keeping it in a separate room, are out of the question. They are way too tempting for these inquisitive cats. If you do get a tree please be careful with the thin strips of foil decoration. Cats love these and will chew on them and they can cause serious damage if swallowed. Do not leave line or string lying around. They love to chew on such things and it can cinch off the intestine and the cat may need surgery. It won't be long before the cub will be up on counters so be careful with hot burners and things left out on the counter. Also if you leave a cup of coffee or a soft drink out you can almost count on having a paw in it in a short period of time.

Some are escape artisst and in no time they can time it so when you open a door to go out they will try to bolt. It is a very good idea to always have two doors between the cat and the outside. Say for instance if you have a patio and it's convenient to go out that way that would be advisable. That way if the cat bolts then he or she is only on the patio and can be caught and put back in the house.

Some people insist on letting the cat roam. This is not a good idea first of all for safety reasons, e.g., stray dogs, cars, etc. And secondly they are very desirable cats and can be stolen easily. If your back yard is fenced it makes no difference. In no time at all the cub will not have a problem negotiating a six foot high fence.

When selecting toys do not get anything that they can chew apart. One lady I know had a rubber spider and the cat chewed the legs off and they became lodged in the intestine and required a few trips to the vet to have them removed. I have spent a lot of money on toys and found out that what they most like to play with is a wadded up piece of newspaper. They will bat it around for hours. Also take an old cardboard box and cut holes in it. They will love to explore and stick their heads out of the different holes. They will also go ballistic over one of the wands that are about two feet long and have either a feather or foil on the end. I have heard them called "ticklers" if you decide to go looking for one.

Also need to mention that these guys love toilet paper for some reason. Although it won't hurt them you may get tired of picking up the mess and running to the store every time you need to use the bathroom.

Well that about sums it up. One thing I like to share with new owner's is that about the time you think he may get into something you left out, it's too late. He will more than likely be already into it. It takes a while to set up a household and adapt to having a wild hybrid but with patience and understanding you will be paid back in spades.

Imagine being taken from your mother before you can even see. Then about the time you can walk and enjoy the company of your siblings, you are locked in a small crate and sent on the most terrifying journey of your young life. It happens in the animal world all the time.

Chapter Seven

Diet and Health Care

Artwork Photo of
"Big Pappa Bear"
A Domestic Stud

I SELDOM, IF EVER, ANSWER INQUIRIES THAT ASK "WHAT IS THE PRICE OF YOUR CATS?" AND NOTHING ELSE.

Chapter Seven

Diet and Health Care

Part One: Diet Considerations

Pure Jungle Cats cannot handle domestic cat food. It will generally give them diarrhea. Most hybrids can handle a good quality, high protein cat food like Eukanaba, Science Diet or Pro Plan. However genetics is never an exact science and occasionally one of the hybrids cannot handle domestic food as it inherited the wild digestive system.

This does not happen very often. I had to find out the hard way. I once placed an F1, 50% wild blood with a family. All of its littermates did fine but this one had diarrhea. After stool samples were run, nothing out of the ordinary was found. The vet, not being familar with wild cat hybrids thought the cub may have irratible bowel syndrome and was about to begin steroid therapy. My vet suggested trying a "bland" first. So I had the owners put the cub on a diet of cooked ground turkey and steamed brown rice. Cook both and use equal parts to feed to the cub. Well the cub cleared up in about one day so this proved to me that he had inherited the wild digestive tract. Incidently this bland diet is great for any pet, cat or dog, if it seems to have an upset stomach. It is not very nutritious but will give the cub's digestive system a chance to return to normal as it is very easy to digest.

Added note: While writing this book I had a gentleman call who got a cat from another breeder. It was an F2 or only 25% wild blood with the same problems mentioned above. It was changed over to the wild feed and cleared up. So even though rare, the diarrhea problem from domestic feeds can happen even with the smaller percentage wild blood cubs. Again by all means, if your animal has diarrhea, first consult a vet. I only list the above as most vets are not familiar with wild blood cats and sometimes it pops up.

If this is the case, after the bland diet, I would recommend feeding it a dry food called Mazuri Wild Feline Small. It is made by Purina Feeds and is a special zoological formula made especially for small wild felines. It is very nutritious and can be eaten by domestic cats also. You generally have to order it from a Purina dealer and it takes about two weeks to get. I pay $25.00 for a 20 pound bag and it will go a long ways. In either case I would highly recommend dry feed over canned. You get a lot more bang for the buck and it will keep plaque from building up on their teeth and avoid future dental problems. You can also give an occasional treat of raw meat but I would do this very sparingly as they may begin to refuse the dry after a while. Raw meat by itself is not very nutritious. Beware! If you are going to feed raw then give it to the cat where it can be alone and do not try to take it back from him for whatever the reason may be. I have seen little docile hybrids get very possessive over a piece of raw meat and growl like lions. If you have two cats and think that if you give each of them a piece it will work, it won't. I have seen them eat a piece and keep one of their paws on another piece to protect it until they can get to it. A lot of owners like to feed and watch the cat eat raw because it makes them look more "wild," if you will. However, if you must feed raw do it with caution. Incidently, feeding raw does not make a cat agressive as according to some myths. Once the cub is done eating the raw meat it will return to its "pre-raw" behavior.

It is a good idea to add a vitamin supplement and one of the best that I have found is one made by the Wysong Company in Midland, Michigan. It is called "Call of the Wild" and is loaded with all kinds of naturally occurring digestive enzymes, many vitamins and nutrients to build the immune system, promote growth, and build strong bodies. You can order it on line from

Revival Animal Products at
http://www.revivalanimal.com

or you can purchase it directly from Wysong Corporation at:
http://ighawaii.com/naturally/wysong/supplement.html

Or you can call them directly at (517) 631-0009

Below is a blurb about the product:

"Dog & cat supplement designed to balance fresh meat meals. Helps achieve archetypal feeding patterns by providing organ meat, fats, connective tissue proteoglycans, minerals, vitamins, enzymes, probiotics, herbs & other micronutrients in the levels & proportions found in natural prey. Probiotics & oligosaccharides help prevent food-borne illness from raw foods."

Although "Call of the Wild" was made specifically to supplement a raw diet it is an excellent additive regardless of what you are feeding. Below is a list of ingredients:

INGREDIENTS: Poultry, Poultry Liver, Dried Whey, Calcite, Ground Bone, Calcium Carbonate, Barley Grass Powder, Wheat Grass Powder, Ground Sesame Seeds, Lecithin, Dried Kelp, Dried Seaweed Meal, Dried Lactobacillus acidophilus Fermentation Product, Dried Lactobacillus casei Fermentation Product, Dried Lactobacillus lactis Fermentation Product, Dried Lactobacillus plantarum Fermentation Product, Dried Entercococcus faecium Fermentation Product, Dried Saccharomyces cerevisiae Fermentation Product, Dried Aspergillus oryzae Fermentation Product, Dried Aspergillus niger Fermentation Product, Phytase, Garlic, Artichoke, Natural Extractives of Sage and Rosemary, Choline Chloride, Ascorbic Acid, Zinc Proteinate, Iron Proteinate, Vitamin E Supplement, Niacin Supplement, Manganese Proteinate, Calcium Pantothenate, Thiamine Mononitrate, Copper Proteinate, Pyridoxine Hydrochloride, Riboflavin Supplement, Vitamin A Acetate, Folic Acid, Biotin, Vitamin B12 Supplement, Vitamin D3 Supplement.

ANALYSIS: Protein 18% Fiber 16% Fat 5% Moisture 10%

Wysong specializes in "all natural" ingredients. As you can see from the above ingredients list that the product is "loaded." As you can see it looks like an inventory from a health food store. At the time of writing this book the cost for a twelve ounce jar was about fourteen dollars. It goes a long way as you only need a small amount sprinkled on each meal. I would venture to guess that if you are supplement-ing only one hybrid that one jar should last two to three months. That is a small price to pay to insure the health and immune system of your cat. If you are feeding dry food you can moisten the food slightly with a hand pump atomizer before sprinkling on the additive and it will stick to the food. You can buy the spray bottles at most discount stores. I would not use anything that previously held any type of product. My cats will eat the Call of the Wild by itself as it is very palatable.

I am in no way making any money off the above product. I just happen to believe in it from personal experience. Is is probably the most expensive supplement out there but I believe it is by far the best one available. Most other supplements I have found may be a lot cheaper but they are either malt or yeast based and the main ingredient is the base and very little nutrient additives.

Part Two. Health Care

Health Care is really quite simple. They get the same health care as a domestic cat would. They receive the same shots except it is recommended that the "Killed" vaccines be used. Make sure and tell this to your veterinarian. A lot of breeders, whether domestic or wild hybrids choose not to give the feline leukemia vaccine. It is a very strong vaccine and has been reported to cause tumors in some cases. If your cat is not allowed to roam, as it should not, then there is no need for it.

Declawing

I do not recommend declawing. It is really an amputation to the first joint. Cats need to be able to dig their claws into something to properly stretch and exercise tendons and muscles. There is information all over the internet against this practice. If you have ample scratching posts and encourage your cat to use them them clawing should not be a problem.

Spaying and Neutering

A lot of veterinarians now will do early spaying and neutering. It used to be that the cat had to be six months old but with the development of safer anesthetics they are doing it much younger. Young kittens also seem to heal faster than adults and are less traumatized by the surgery. However this is fine with spaying but early neutering can affect the physical development of the males. Disproportionate head to body size has been reported in a fair number of "early neutered" males. So I would recommend waiting until five to six months to get a male neutered.

Other Considerations: Emergency Supplies.

Due to the wild blood hybrids are, on the whole, very healthy and robust animals. But as with children, even the healthiest can get sick from time to time. Let me emphasize that this is rare but I would be prepared. Cats, especially the young kittens and cubs, do not have a very large reserve of fluids. It seems like, if anything affects them, one of the first signs is diarrhea. Fluid loss can cause electrolyte imbalance which will only add to the dilemma. They can have a significant fluid loss in very little time and become lethargic and then not want to eat and the problem only compounds.

It is very easy to check for proper hydration in a cat. If when pinch a fold of skin at the back of the neck and then let go it should fall back into place easily. If the cat is dehydrated the skin will remain folded together and be slow to return to normal almost like it's stuck together. The eyes should be clear and not look "filmy."

I would keep a couple of cans of Pedialyte on hand as it will restore fluid and it is good for electrolyte replacement. If the cat will not take it on its own then I would administer it with a syringe. A 6cc syringe will suffice. To give it to the cat, sit down and place a towel on your lap. Next, place the cat on your lap and get a firm hold of the skin on the back of the neck. They are normally picked up this way by the mother and have few nerve endings in this area. Tilt the head sideways and then trickle the fluid in between the cheek and gum on the side of the jaw that is the lowest or the closest to your lap. He or she will automatically start lapping it up. Give small amounts each time but give it often. For example a three to four pound cub could easily take 15cc's every hour. Do not force the fluid. Too much at once and the cat may aspirate. Go slowly and easily just letting it trickle in. You can also take the ingedients for the aforementioned bland diet and place a small amount in a blender with enough Pediolyte so that it will puree easily. When that is done you can strain it through a fine mesh wire strainer and then pull it up in a syringe and administer the same way as you did the fluid. Do not mix any vitamin supplement to the bland mix. This will give the pet an excellent chance of a fast recovery. If you have the supplies on hand it is much easier than to run around trying to find them should something occur.

By all means, if your cat shows any signs of any type of illness, I would first try to get it to a vet. The syringe feedings are mentioned only as an aid to recovery and to sustain the cat until you can get it to the vet and not as a cure for anything.

It should be mentioned that mostly all cats, regardless of

how well they are bred and cared for, carry coccidia in their digestive systems. They are "opportunistic" protozoans and can flare up when the immune system is compromised. Both can be exacerbated by stress and cause diarrhea which, if left untreated, can seriously compromise the health of the cat. When a kitten leaves its mother and littermates for the first time and goes to a new home it can put stress on the cat and weaken the immune system enough for the protozoans to multiply and cause diarrhea. This is rare but it can and does happen. A stool sample taken to the vet can detect coccidia. It is easily treatable and I felt worth mentioning.

Chapter Eight

How Big Do They Get?

"Big Jean Cougar"
Up a Tree

At a zoo in India, a cheetah gave birth to a litter next to a cage of baboons, normally mortal enemies in the wild.
One of the cubs would crawl under the fencing and and make regular visits to let the baboon pick parasites off of it.
They bonded and became the best of friends.
He stayed with his mother to be nutrured and still bonded to a totally different species.
Articles like this encouraged my "No Bottle feeding policy."

Chapter Eight

How Big Do They Get?

The size of your hybrid will depend on the size of the cats used by the breeder, both wild and domestic parents. There are several subspecies of Jungle Cat and some do not get all that large. As I have only large cats in my line I regularly get F1 males over twenty-two pounds and females between eighteen and twenty-two pounds. The males are generally about fifteen to twenty percent larger than the females.

If smaller cats are used then I would expect the overall size to be much smaller. Neutering always adds a few pounds to a cat but I have seen full grown, male, Abyssinian, F1 crosses at twelve to thirteen pounds. Again if you are looking for a big cat, ask the breeder for references and then call the owners and ask about size. Ask how big their male Jungle Cat is and how big the female is. The secret to success in getting the cat that you want is to, ask, ask, ask and then ask some more.

I get requests all the time for cats that look like my Jungle Cats Mongo and Bocephus. People love the looks and the size! One way to get both is to get a cat with a high percentage of wild blood, say 75% or 87 1/2% wild blood. However, there are drawbacks to owning a high percentage cub and it will be discussed later on in Chapter 16.

If you want a lap cat then you would have to opt for a lower percentage or perhaps a F2 or F3 but you will more than likely be giving up size and looks. There always seems to be a tradeoff. From what I have seen with those trying to breed chausies your chances of getting an F2 or an F3 to get very large are minimal at best. I suppose that is why I prefer to raise Jungle Cat Hybrids. That way I am not limited to the smaller cats that one has to use to produce chausies. At the time of writing this book we are waiting for Big Papa Bear to sire a litter of F2 Jungle Cat Hybrids. He is a big, thick , stout domestic cat with big meaty paws. He has the feral look and has it all going on. With him, I expect his F2 cubs to have great size, excellent temperaments and a very wild/feral cat look. He has sired a litter of domestics and they are all almost three pounds at only 7 weeks old. And that is with a 12 lb domestic female!!! Can't imagine what will happen when he finally hooks up with one of my big girls!! COME ON BIG PAPA!!!!

Author's note: I have recently rewritten this book and Papa Bear, after almost two years of trying did successfully breed to my female 50% wild cat, PJ Puma and produced one F2 cub. She is beautiful and at the time of writing is 9 weeks old and a very solid, big cub!!!!

Chapter Nine

How Are Their Temperaments?

"Cleo Panther"
A 50% Wild Hybrid
Playing in the Water

BUYING AN ANIMAL
OVER THE INTERNET
AND HAVING IT
FLOWN TO YOU IS
LIKE BUYING A PIG IN
A POKE.

Chapter Nine

How Are Their Temperaments?

The factors affecting temperaments of Chausies and Jungle Cat Hybrids are interchangeable so there is no need to distinguish between the two.

There are several things to look at when considering the the temperament issue. One of the questions I constantly get asked is "Is there any difference in the temperament between a male and a female?" If the cub is reared, socialized properly, spayed or neutered at the appropriate time, I see very little difference between the friendliness of a male or a female.

As a rule they are very active, intelligent and extremely inquisitive cats. They like high places and most seem to be hydrophilic. A lot of them will not hesitate to dive in a tub full of water and love to splash dish water all over. For the first year of their lives they are very active but seem to mellow out after reaching one year of age or about that time.

The percentage of wild blood can affect the temperaments also. The higher percentage hybrids, F1's or fifty percent wild blood if reared properly and given a lot of attention make good pets. Most love to be played with and love attention. Most can be taught to fetch in a short time. However, on the whole they are not lap cats and do not like to be picked up and held for any length of time. F2's or twenty-five percent wild blood cats and lower, depending on the out cross domestic used, are still active and intelligent but have a lot more of the domestic traits and many can become lap cats and love to be held. The "Catch 22" here is, if you want a larger cat you generally have to get an F1. Most F2's unless specifically bred for size can be of only average size. That is generally the trade off. A better temperament for less size. I have bred many F1's that have gotten very large and have made good pets but as stated they are definitely not lap cats. So it's a judgement call depending on the purchaser's preferences. I have spent a lot of money on studs and kept only my biggest females in an effort to keep size in my line.

The temperaments of high percentage cubs, greater than 50%, will be discussed in detail in Chapter 16.

Chapter Ten

License and Permits

A Beautiful
Wild Hybrid
Polydactyl Cub

OWNING A WILD HYBRID
IS A MAJOR LIFESTYLE
CHANGE.
THERE ARE THOSE WHO ARE
ABSOLUTELY FANATICAL
ABOUT THEM AND THOSE
WHO SHOULDN'T OWN ONE.

Chapter Ten

License and Permits

To the best of my knowledge the only states where hybrids are illegal are Georgia and Connecticut. You also need to check city and county ordinances. It has been my experience though that if you call one of these facilities they will have no idea what you are talking about. In most instances in all of the other states no special license or permit is required.

In most states, to the best of my knowledge, the percentage of wild blood is not an issue either. Even the very high percentage wild blooded hybrids are still considered hybrids and in most cases permits or special licenses are not required. Again, it is up to the owner to check state and local laws as these can change all the time.

THE AIRLINE COMPANIES
REFUSE TO MAKE AVAILABLE
TO THE PUBLIC RECORDS
CONCERNING ANIMALS THAT
ARE KILLED OR INJURED
WHILE IN THEIR CARE.

WHAT COULD THEY
POSSIBLY BE TRYING TO
HIDE?

Chapter Eleven

Relatively Inexpensive Caging Ideas

Outside Caging

EMAIL WRITTEN BY NEW PARENT:
CHUCK, I WILL BE FLYING DOWN TO GET MY CUB. I TOTALLY AGREE WITH YOUR "NO SHIPPING" POLICY. I WORK AS BAGGAGE HANDLER XXXXX AIRLINES. THANKS, JD FROM MINNESOTA

Chapter Eleven

Relatively Inexpensive Caging Ideas

Although I am against the caging of an animal I believe it is great for them to have an outside play area to burn off energy. Also when they are younger and tearing around, sometimes it's nice to have a little break from these guys.

If you wish to have the cat fairly well secluded from view you may choose a method we use here at Mandala Exotic Cats. As you view the pictures in this book you can get an idea of what the finished product will look like and below is a material list. This is enough material to build an eight foot wide by six foot high by sixteen foot long outside play area. The plans may seem a bit vague to some but I am just giving you a rough idea as to size, cost, etc. If you wish more detailed information you may email me at cmongo2345@aol.com

Item	Quantity	.......Approx.Cost
6' X 8" wood fence panel	6	$150.00
4" X 4" wood posts	6	30.00
2" X 4" X 16' pine	2	. 10.00
2" X 4" X 8" pine	5	.. 26.00
8' X 16' chain link (11 gauge)	1	.. 32.00

1 lb. of 3 1/2" galvanized deck screws	1	3.50
1 lb fencing nails	1	1.00
Misc. door hinges, hasp, etc		10.00

Total cost	$ 262.50

Once you have been to the lumber yard and spent your hard earned money, the worst part is over. At least the most painful part is. To begin with you will need to sink the 4 X 4 support posts in an eight foot by sixteen foot rectangle. Two on either end of the eight foot ends and one in the middle of the sixteen foot long sections. You can get a book at the lumber yard such as Home Depot that will show you how to square the base so the fencing panels will fit nicely. Once the layout is squared and the posts are sunken in the ground and the dirt tamped around them you can screw on the fencing panels. I like to use galvanized wood screws for all the cage framing. They hold the framing material together much better than nails. Once the panels are secured in place then you can cut in the door and hinge it with some heavy duty galvanized wood screws. Attach the hasp to use as a locking device.

Next you need to construct the wood frame for the roof. I find it easier if I build them on the ground and then get help to hoist them into place. Off to one side of the fenced in part lay out the two sixteen foot 2 x 4's approximately eight feet apart on edge. Between them and at a ninety degree angle you will need to lay out the cross members which will be the 2 x 4 x 8 foot pine pieces. Place one on either end and the others will be spaced four feet apart and screwed in place. Make sure the frame is square and place a temporary brace to hold it square if you need to. Next roll the chain link over the top of the completed roof framing. Nail one end and go to the other end and while someone stretches the chain link you can nail the other end to help keep it somewhat taut. It does not have to be very tight, just enough to take up some of the slack. Two to three people should be able to easily lift the completed roof panel over the top of the fencing and screw it to the top with the wood screws. You may want to place some chunks of 2 x 4 on the inside of the fencing for temporary support for the roof frame until you can screw the framing in place. I realize that I have simplified these plans somewhat but this should give you a working knowledge on how to build one. Next you can add some big tree limbs and possibly an inside shelter with a roof to keep out the rain. In the summer you can add a kiddie swimming pool. I have one that I fill with water and then put in chunks of tree limbs that I cut about two inches long and throw them in. The cats will spend hours trying to get them out.

DOGS COME WHEN YOU CALL.
CATS TAKE YOUR
NUMBER AND WILL GET
BACK WITH YOU LATER.

Chapter Twelve

A Sample Health Guarantee

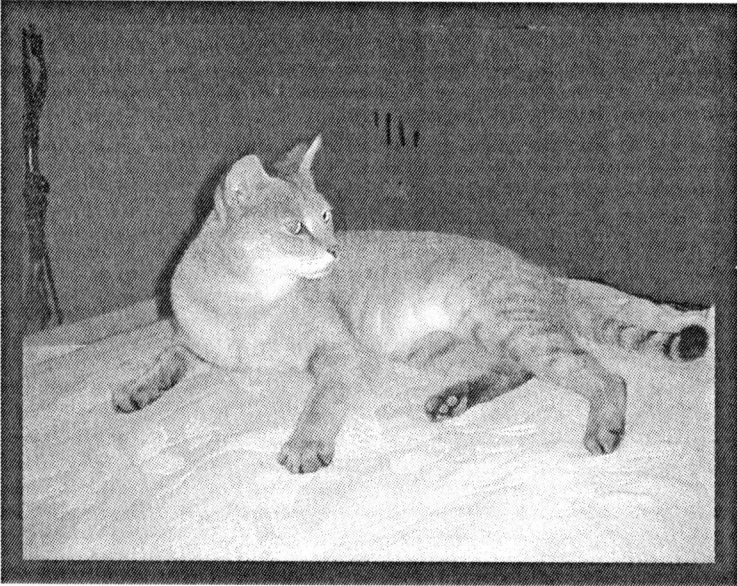

"Mongo the Bondsman"
The Most Beautiful
Jungle Cat in the World.
Resides at Mandala Exotic Cats
Sarasota, Florida

GOD MADE THE CAT
IN ORDER THAT MAN
MIGHT HAVE THE
PLEASURE OF
CARESSING THE

LION

Chapter Twelve

A Sample Health Guarantee

Health guarantees for pets vary from state to state but generally cover the same basic areas. Below is a copy of Statute 828 governing the sale of cats in Florida. If you read it you will get a general idea of most health laws in the United States and familiarize youself with health terminology. Basically it states what most laws state governing the sale of animals and that is you have only several business days to have the cat examined by a veterinarian and if anything is found to be wrong the breeder is obligated to replace the cat or cover veterinarian expenses up to the price of the cat. Usually you have up to one year on congenital conditions that can be proven to have existed at birth. It would be wise to ask your veterinarian or state office for a copy.

FL 828
(b) For each cat offered for sale within the state, the tests, vaccines, and anthelmintics required by this section must be administered by or under the direction of a veterinarian, licensed by the state and accredited by the United States Department of Agriculture, who issues the official certificate of veterinary inspection. The tests, vaccines, and anthelmintics must be administered before the cat is offered for sale in the state, unless the licensed, accredited veterinarian certifies on the official certificate of veterinary inspection that to inoculate or deworm the cat is not in the best medical interest of the cat, in which case the vaccine or anthelmintic may not be administered to that particular cat.

Each cat must receive vaccines and anthelmintics against the following diseases and internal parasites:

1. Panleukopenia.

2. Feline viral rhinotracheitis.

3. Calici virus.

4. Rabies, if the cat is over 3 months of age and the inoculation is administered by a licensed veterinarian.

5. Hookworms.

6. Roundworms.

Vaccines, and anthelmintics required by this section must be administered no more than 21 days before sale within the state. If the cat is 4 months of age or older, the tests, vaccines, and anthelmintics required by this section must be administered at or after 3 months of age, but no more than 1 year before sale within the state.

(3)(a) Each dog or cat subject to subsection (1) or subsection (2) must be accompanied by a current official certificate of veterinary inspection at all times while being offered for sale within the state. The examining veterinarian must retain one copy of the official certificate of veterinary inspection on file for at least 1 year after the date of examination. At the time of sale of the animal, one copy of the official certificate of veterinary inspection must be given to the buyer. The seller must retain one copy of the official certificate of veterinary inspection on record for at least 1 year after the date of sale.

(b)   The term "official certificate of veterinary inspection" means a legible certificate of veterinary inspection signed by the examining veterinarian licensed by the state of origin and accredited by the United States Department of Agriculture, that shows the age, sex, breed, color, and health record of the dog or cat, the printed or typed names and addresses of the person or business from whom the animal was obtained, the consignor or seller, the consignee or purchaser, and the examining veterinarian, and the veterinarian's license number. The official certificate of veterinary inspection must list all vaccines and deworming medications administered to the dog or cat, including the manufacturer, vaccine, type, lot number, expiration date, and the dates of administration thereof, and must state that the examining veterinarian warrants that, to the best of his or her knowledge, the animal has no sign of contagious or infectious diseases and has no evidence of internal or external parasites, including coccidiosis and ear mites, but excluding fleas and ticks. The Department of Agriculture and Consumer Services shall supply the official intrastate certificate of veterinary inspection required by this section at cost.

(c) The examination of each dog and cat by a veterinarian must take place no more than 30 days before the sale within the state. The examination must include, but not be limited to, a fecal test to determine if the dog or cat is free of internal parasites, including hookworms, roundworms, tapeworms, and whipworms. If the examination warrants, the dog or cat must be treated with a specific anthelmintic. In the absence of a definitive parasitic diagnosis, each dog or cat must be given a broad spectrum anthelmintic.

Each dog over 6 months of age must also be tested for heart-worms. Each cat must also be tested for feline leukemia before being offered for sale in the state. All of these tests must be performed by or under the supervision of a licensed veterinarian, and the results of the tests must be listed on the official certificate of veterinary inspection.

(d) All dogs and cats offered for sale and copies of certificates held by the seller and veterinarian are subject to inspection by any agent of the Department of Agriculture and Consumer Services, any agent of the United States Department of Agriculture, any law enforcement officer, or any agent appointed under s. 828.03.

(4) A person may not transport into the state for sale or offer for sale within the state any dog or cat that is less than 8 weeks of age.

(5) If, within 14 days following the sale by a pet dealer of an animal subject to this section, a licensed veterinarian of the consumer's choosing certifies that, at the time of the sale, the animal was unfit for purchase due to illness or disease, the presence of symptoms of a contagious or infectious disease, or the presence of internal or external parasites, excluding fleas and ticks or if, within 1 year following the sale of an animal subject to this section, a licensed veterinarian of the consumer's choosing certifies such animal to be unfit for purchase due to a congenital or hereditary disorder which adversely affects the health of the animal or if, within 1 year following the sale of an animal subject to this section, the breed, sex, or health of such animal is found to have been

misrepresented to the consumer, the pet dealer shall afford the consumer the right to choose one of the following options:

(a) The right to return the animal and receive a refund of the purchase price, including the sales tax, and reimbursement for reasonable veterinary costs directly related to the veterinarian's examination and certification that the dog or cat is unfit for purchase pursuant to this section and directly related to necessary emergency services and treatment undertaken to relieve suffering

(b) The right to return the animal and receive an exchange dog or cat of the consumer's choice of equivalent value, and reimbursement for reasonable veterinary costs directly related to the veterinarian's examination and certification that the dog or cat is unfit for purchase pursuant to this section and directly related to necessary emergency services and treatment undertaken to relieve suffering or

(c) The right to retain the animal and receive reimbursement for reasonable veterinary costs for necessary services and treatment related to the attempt to cure or curing of the dog or cat.

Reimbursement for veterinary costs may not exceed the purchase price of the animal. The cost of veterinary services is reasonable if comparable to the cost of similar services rendered by other licensed veterinarians in proximity to the treating veterinarian and the services rendered are appropriate for the certification by the veterinarian.

(6) A consumer may sign a waiver relinquishing his or her

right to return the dog or cat for congenital or hereditary disorders. In the case of such waiver, the consumer has 48 normal business hours, excluding weekends and holidays, in which to have the animal examined by a licensed veterinarian of the consumer's choosing. If the veterinarian certifies that, at the time of sale, the dog or cat was unfit for purchase due to a congenital or hereditary disorder, the pet dealer must afford the consumer the right to choose one of the following options:

(a) The right to return the animal and receive a refund of the purchase price, including sales tax, but excluding the veterinary costs related to the certification that the dog or cat is unfit or

(b) The right to return the animal and receive an exchange dog or cat of the consumer's choice of equivalent value, but not a refund of the veterinary costs related to the certification that the dog or cat is unfit.

(7) A pet dealer may specifically state at the time of sale, in writing to the consumer, the presence of specific congenital or hereditary disorders, in which case the consumer has no right to any refund or exchange for those disorders.

(8) The refund or exchange required by subsection (5) or subsection (6) shall be made by the pet dealer not later than 10 business days following receipt of a signed veterinary certification as required in subsection (5) or subsection (6). The consumer must notify the pet dealer within 2 business days after the veterinarian's determination that the animal is unfit. The written certification of unfitness must be presented to the pet dealer not later than 3 business days following

receipt thereof by the consumer.

(9) An animal may not be determined unfit for sale on account of an injury sustained or illness contracted after the consumer takes possession of the animal. A veterinary finding of intestinal or external parasites is not grounds for declaring a dog or cat unfit for sale unless the animal is clinically ill because of that condition.

SHIPPING AN AMIMAL
"COUNTER TO COUNTER"
IS VIRTUALLY THE SAME
THING AS SHIPPING
"CARGO."
THEY ALL END UP IN THE
SAME PLACE. IN AN UNAT-
TENDED, DARK, AND FRIGHT-
ENING CARGO BAY OF AN
AIRCRAFT.

Chapter Thirteen

Litter Box Issues

**Artwork Photo
of
"Big Pappa Bear"**

"A CAT'S EYES ARE WINDOWS
ENABLING US TO SEE INTO
ANOTHER WORLD."
IRISH LEGEND

One of the major concerns with people looking into the hybrids is litter box usage. First of all prospective owners want to know "if" they use the litter box and secondly "how big" of a box do they need.

Chausies and Jungle Cat Hybrids are very easily litter box trained and should be using the box regularly by the time they are eight weeks of age. Even my pure jungle cats use the litter box when in the house.

There may be times when they choose not to use the litter box. When they first get to a new home they may take a few days to adapt as with any other cat and choose not to use the box. If he or she should do this, pick up the waste and place it in the box so that the cub knows to go there. You also may want to place a litter box where it chose to do it's duty. This is a very rare occurrence however.

I have also seen them quit using the litter box as a way to "act out." One gentleman purchased a hybrid from me and called about two weeks later and said that his cub had stopped using the litter box. After some conversation I found out that he worked all day and the cub was alone for up to ten hours by himself. I had told him previously, like all the others that they must have companionship. He stated that a room mate would be moving in shortly and she had a cat. I called him back a month later; the room mate had moved in and brought her cat for company and all was fine.

Our cubs get quite large and quickly outgrow a regular sized litter box. After about 4 months old I use a plastic storage bin. They can be purchased at most discount stores for about $5.00 each. I use a good sized one about 24" long by 16" wide and 14" deep. I would buy two of them. Then get a plastic grocery basket. They are the kind that all supermarkets have that you carry if you are only getting a few things. They have many slots and make a great sifter. I purchased mine from a hardware store that had too many. If not you can find them on line by simply putting "grocery baskets, plastic" in the search window. In one of the bins you can add about 25 pounds of clumpable litter. The next morning place the basket in the clean litter box and dump the used litter in the basket and then lift the basket out shaking gently. The unused litter will fall through into the clean bin and the clumps will stay in the basket. Then dump the clumps back into the first bin that you just emptied. If you don't do this some loose litter will fall out of the basket and make a mess. Then dump the bin with the clumps into a waste receptacle. It may sound technical and time consuming but once you have done it a couple of times the whole process takes about a minute and is much faster and more sanitary then digging through the litter with a hand sifter.

Once this is done you can rinse out the used bin and let it dry for the next day.

Chapter Fourteen

Leash and Fetch Training

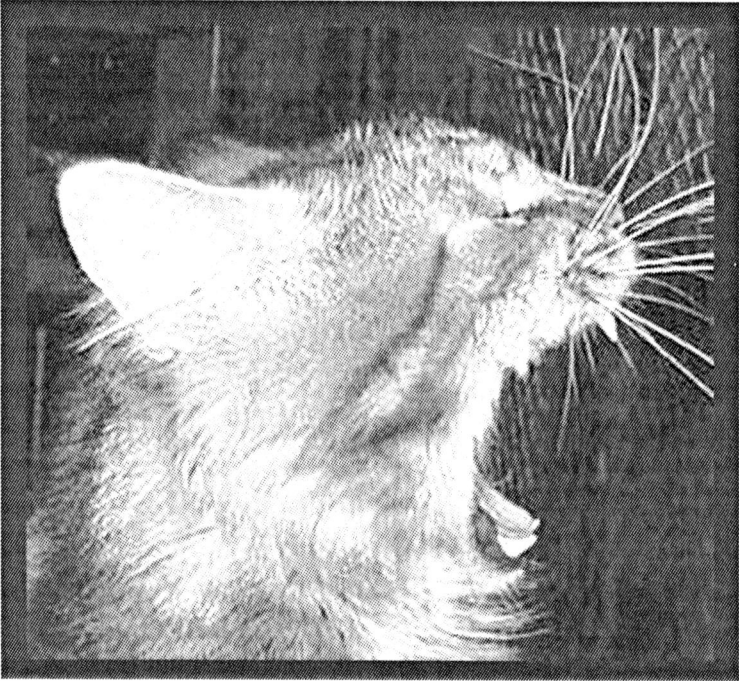

"Big Pappa Bear"
Waking up

A CAT
IS A
LION
IN A JUNGLE OF
SMALL
BUSHES
INDIAN SAYING

Chapter Fourteen

Leash and Fetch Training

I have had several owners choose to leash train their cubs. They love to take them for walks and as one owner claims "There is no better therapy for our cub than a long walk."

The main thing to do is to start very young. Buy a small harness from one of the many pet stores. Get one that fits. It will outgrow it soon but that is much better than buying one that is too big and it either escapes or chafes itself on a poorly fitting harness. There are two kinds available. One is in the shape of a figure eight with one loop going over the head and the other around the mid-section. I do not like these. They do not fit snugly around the neck and go down from the neck in a v-shape. It is too easy for them to get out of this kind and they are very agile and can get their front legs out of it and even if it doesn't escape it's a hassle stopping constantly to fix and readjust the harness. The other type looks almost like two collars that are joined by a piece of harness material. Where the collar that goes around the mid-section meets the joining strip there is a D-ring for attaching the lead. These are very easy to adjust to the animal and offer no chance of escape. After your cub is home and adjusted to the new family members you can start by putting the harness on the cub and just letting him wear it around. At first it may act like it's uncomfortable but he will get used to it in no time at all. The main ingredient is patience. They are not dogs and do not readily accept a leash as fast as a dog will. Once he is used to the smell and fit of the harness you can then attach the lead. In a safe place, like your back yard, let him walk wherever he chooses with you following and holding on to the lead. Keep this up for several weeks. Then slowly introduce him to being led by you. They are easily distracted and will want to run off and chase anything that moves like bugs or birds so you have to take your time.

If you are going to take your hybrid out of the back yard you must make certain there are NO dogs in the area. One pet owner takes along some pepper spray and a carrier in case they encounter a potentially dangerous situation. If the cub should get frightened for whatever reason they can put him in the carrier for the trip back home. Remember it's a whole new, scary world to them and their safety is utmost.

As far as fetching goes I find that about one half of my hybrids adapt readily to it and it seems like the most natural thing in the world to them. As long as you are willing to toss an object that they can pick up, they are more than happy to retrieve it for you for hours on end. On the other hand, there are those that simply are not interested and there seems to be no way you can make them do it. To try to force a hybrid to do "anything" is an exercise in futility.

Chapter Fifteen

Bottle Feeding Information

"Mamma Cass"
A Beautiful F2
Jungle Cat Hybrid
At Eight Weeks of age.

"THERE ARE PEOPLE WHO
RESHAPE THE WORLD BY
FORCE OR ARGUMENT BUT
THE CAT JUST LIES THERE,
DOZING, AND THE WORLD
QUIETLY RESHAPES ITSELF
TO SUIT HIS COMFORT AND
CONVENIENCE."
ALAN AND IVY DODD

Chapter Fifteen

Bottle Feeding Information

I have been breeding Jungle Cat Hybrids for some time now and have placed many over the years in great homes. When I first started I had to learn everything from scratch from other breeders. Common practice at that time was to "pull" the young cubs from the mother and bottle feed them. Different breeders pulled at different ages ranging from 5-10 days normally. The common thought of the day was that if you didn't take them from the mother they would not bond to humans and would become mean and unmanageable. Well, intending to do the proper thing I had my first litter and was very excited. I took the cubs from their mother at 10 days old and she immediately starting pacing and crying. If kept away long enough she will go through a period of grief and then come back into heat believing she has lost the litter. Well this lasted about two hours with me and I simply put the cubs back with the mother as I couldn't take it any longer. I had made my bed and figured that if they became mean because of it, I would just have to keep them all and pursue another field. However, the mom was an excellent mom and would let me handle the cubs all the time. I was determined to handle them all I could when the mom was not nursing or cleaning them. She didn't mind the break at all. I would put them in bed with me and play with them until mom got ready to take them back or they fell asleep. I continued with this practice day after day, spending as much time as reasonably possible and much to my surprise they became very friendly and outgoing. Well, that litter was quickly placed in new homes and did great and are doing great to this day. The new owners loved them and they got along well with humans as well as other cats and dogs. So, thank God...the experiment worked!!!!! They received the best of both worlds. They got the constant around the clock nurturing and feeding from mom and all the human contact I could possibly give them. I continue this practice to this day and have had excellent results. Listed below are some myths I have seen on other sites and would like to share my experience with you.

Myth Number One: If the kittens are not bottle fed and pulled from their mother, they will not bond to humans and will become mean. As stated above, this is simply not true. I read in a zoological review where, at a zoo in India a litter of cheetahs was born and in the next cage was a litter of baboons. Mortal enemies to the cheetah in the wild. One little cheetah cub managed to worm his way under the fence and would go and visit a female baboon. Well instead of killing the little guy she started grooming him and picking fleas off of him. When she was done and he got hungry, he would sneak back under the fence to mom. The two bonded nicely and became great friends. Now if this bonding can happen with mortal enemies, it surely can and does happen with human/hybrid relationships.

Myth Number Two: If they are not bottle fed they will quit using the litter box later on in life. I cannot for the life of me figure out where this idea came from. Studies dictate quite

The Jungle Cat Hybrid and Chausie Manual

the opposite.

Some other reasons why we choose not to bottle feed.

1.) There is NO substitute for mother's milk. Nutritionally, Mother Nature still knows best.

2.) Kittens take on the mother's immunity to diseases through her milk.

3.) There is NO substitute for a mother's care. If you have EVER watched a queen taking care of her cubs, you would know exactly what I was referring to.

4.) The cubs develop much better emotionally and mentally. I think we have all heard tons of stories about children who are not nurtured as babies. The newspapers are full of such accounts. I believe it is the same in the animal world. The early days of nurturing are extremely important.

I am not against bottle feeding if that is what other breeders choose to do and am in no way saying that if a cub is not bottle fed he or she will end up unhandlable. Just stating my reasons for not choosing not to bottle feed as there seems to be so much misinformation out there regarding this issue.

91

A
CAT WILL
BE YOUR
FRIEND,
BUT NEVER YOUR
SLAVE

Chapter Sixteen

High Percentage Wild Hybrids

A 75% Wild Hybrid
Just Playing
Around

CATS
SEEM TO GO ON
THE PRINCIPLE
THAT IT NEVER DOES ANY
HARM TO ASK FOR WHAT
YOU
WANT

Chapter Sixteen

High Percentage Wild Hybrids

In talking about high percentage wild hybrids I am going to try to be as honest as I can but speak from my own personal experience. The opinions expressed herein are mine only.

In breeding as with everything else I believe that one has to learn from experience. At first I was told it was great to ship cats by air and found out later that it is not good at all and stopped the practice. I was also told that "line breeding" is commonly practiced in the breeding world and it doesn't affect the outcome of the litters. "Line breeding" is when a sire is bred back to a daughter or a son back to a mother. Another term would be "inbreeding." A lot of new breeds are started this way. For example lets say that a kitten is born with some type of genetic mutation that doesn't affect its health but is a desireable trait or a new trait someone wishes to propagate. I believe that the hairless and some curly coated cats were begun by this method. For example let's say a breeder has a cat with an unusual coat that is very rare and they wish to have more kittens with the same trait or wish to start a whole new breed based on this variation. About the only way to insure this variation will reproduce is to linebreed or inbreed a male kitten back to the mother. What I am trying to show here is that it is a commom practice.

Many times a high percentage hybrid (greater than 50%) is the result of linebreeding or inbreeding as most breeders have only one one Jungle Cat stud. For instance, let's suppose that a pure male Jungle is bred to a domestic. The offspring would be F1's or fifty percent wild blood. Now if the breeder wanted to go higher in percentage of wild blood they would line breed the sire back to one of the daughters and the resultant offspring would be 75% wild blood. I have done this in the past and had about three litters of 75% wild blood. I spent a ton of time with them and did all I could to socialize them. All were fine when they were here at the cattery. However out of the fifteen high percentage (75%) cats I started to get emails from the new owners. I would venture to guess that about ten of them fared quite well and made excellent, wild looking pets. All of them looked very wild and got quite large. However, two of them ended up unhandlable. Two more of them preferred male companionship only as they were handled by me only and tolerated females but didn't want a whole lot to do with them. I sold one absolutely stunning, 75% wild blooded to a lady that waited a long time to get him. He was a bit of a rascal when he was here but very friendly and outgoing. She got him home and he wanted little to do with her. Her grown son came over and the cub went crazy over him. She gave the cub to the gentleman and they have been as thick as thieves since.

I guess you could argue that the greater percentage turned out to be acceptable cats and that is sufficient. However I do not want to see one cat not get along well. I surmised, and I have no proof, that the aberrant behavior was the result of line breeding and have stopped the practice. I have since acquired a second pure male Jungle Cat that is totally unrelated to my line and will be using him for higher percentage cats. I believe this will correct the several behavior problems that I have encountered but at the time this book was written the new male was still too young to mate so the jury is still out on my theory.

UPDATE: This is the revised copy of The Jungle Cat Hybrid Manual and as I have stated earlier I have to live and learn. Since writing the original version I had repeat request for cats out of Mongo so I bred one more time and had two litters. I was going to really put the time in and see if line breeding did, in fact, affect the temperaments. I had two litters of 75% wild in the fall of 2002. I used to wait until their eyes were open (10-15 days old) to start handling them. Well, this time I handled them from day one and virtually lived with them 24/7 until they left. I had twelve cubs in the two litters and had my hands full! Well, they all came out great, went to new homes, and had virtually no problems adapting to new homes. I have seen many domestics do a lot worse than these guys. I was very proud of them.

I get requests constantly for golden hybrid cats that look like the big males that I have and most people want cats that will get big. The high percentage hybrids, of course, have a much greater chance in filling this bill than any other.

I would be cautious before deciding about purchasing a cat with more than 50% wild blood. Also the high percentage cubs are not for everyone or for every situation. For the most part it will be like raising a pure Jungle Cat. If you have read Chapter One entitled "What Is a Jungle Cat?" I talk about owning one and keeping it in the house. They can wreak havoc on a place especially when young. My two pure Jungle Cats are in the house almost every night and have mellowed considerably and sleep with me and I enjoy them thoroughly. However, I have the deepest respect for them. They can be very loving but need their space. They will let you know when they want to be petted and when they wish to be left alone. Everything is on their terms! If you are a "control freak" these are definitely not for you. You have to get to know the cat and its looks. They will signal with a certain look that tells you that they wish to be left alone and the best thing to do is to leave them alone. On the other hand, the understanding between me and Mongo for instance, I wouldn't trade for the world. He has taught me a lot about the wild cat.

If you have children I would not recommend a high percentage cat unless your children are older and very respectful of animals in general. They can do some things that are very unnerving. Sometimes, when they want to be petted or want attention, they will put their mouth on your arm and bite down gently. This is not an aggressive maneuver but they can be very oral in their request. To the untrained observer or a child this could be very frightening and cause the child to pull back and cause harm. Also if a child gets wound up and begins running around the cub will love it but the prey instinct can kick in and the child may get jumped on. Even if this is in a playful mode, which it usually is, a child can get frightened and escalate the cat's behavior.

I do not recommend any type of wild cat being owned by people with smaller children nor will I knowingly sell one to people that still have little ones at home. Even under the best of circumstances a cat could get stepped on accidently and try to defend itself so it is not a good idea.

On the other, if you have researched the breed and believe that a high percentage cat will fill the bill for you, you will get to experience the majesty of a wild cat up close and personal.

Chapter Seventeen

A Breeder's Story

"Mongo the Bondsman"
of
Mandala Exotic Cats
One Last Time

GOOD FRIENDS ARE
HARD TO FIND.
THEY ARE LOYAL TO
A FAULT AND
FORGIVE IN AN
INSTANT.
MOST OF THEM HAVE
FOUR LEGS

Chapter Seventeen

A Breeder's Story

Author's note: Decided to add this chapter just for leisure reading. However, I am very prejudiced and believe it to be an interesting and heartwarming story. Hahahaha, enjoy.

Having been bengal breeders for some time we became interested in exotic cats and decided to do some research. Although we loved the bengal breed and still do we wanted to produce a cat similar to the bengal but much larger. What we had hoped to accomplish was to breed a large wild looking cat with a domestic temperament. A HUGE house hybrid was and still is our goal.

Looking into the new chausie breed we decided that the Jungle Cat would give us the size and the wild looks. We could add the body type hopefully by using certain, carefully selected domestic cats as crosses.

We located a cat breeder in central Florida that had Jungle Cats and put in our order. It would be a while before he would be born so in the meantime we set out to find a suitable female to begin our chausie breeding program. We were very fortunate to locate a cat breeder in Minnesota that had the same goals in mind that we had. She had a foundation kitten that was out of a 20 lb. female Pixe Bob and an 18 lb. male Maine Coon. The kitten was also a polydactyl (extra toed) which meant she would carry heavy boning. Although she was a marble coat, she carried the heavy, long and low body type we were looking for. Her name was "Peepers" and we sent for her immediately.

Peepers the future chausie queen had been with us for some time when Mongo was born. We were very excited to say the least. He was the only male in his litter and thus began the longest 8 weeks of our lives waiting for our new little Jungle Cat. There were many calls to the breeder checking on his progress and two trips to the breeder's cattery to check him out.

Finally the day came and the breeder called and said that he was ready to come home. I flew to the breeder's, a 150 mile drive and picked up my little three pound Jungle Cat. As soon as I got him home I noticed two things. One was that he had a cough and diarrhea. The other was that he was very ill tempered. He would try to scratch and bite if you tried to pet him or pick him up. We figured we could deal with the temperament problems later but needed to get him to the vet immediately. The vet ran a flea comb through his fur and noticed he was loaded with fleas. I had started him on a flea control program the the day before so that problem was solved. The vet couldn't understand the coughing but put him on an antibiotic for safety's sake with instructions to get back in 10 days. Well, after 10 days the coughing continued and the diarrhea stayed off and on. The vet said that he probably had a throat obstruction and I was to bring him back three days later on a Monday to give him an anesthetic and he would look down his throat.

The Saturday before the vet appointment his coughing worsened and luckily the vet I had been seeing was closed so I selected another vet at random out of the phone book. The new vet x-rayed him immediately, which should have been done a long time ago and gave me a very poor prognosis. He said "You have a very,very sick Jungle Cat. He has pneumonia and 90% of his lungs are infiltrated and he is only breathing out of the top of his lobes." I mentioned that the other vet thought he had a throat obstruction and he was going to be put under on Monday and have his throat looked at. The new vet stated that he never would have made it through the sedation in his condition.He administered IM antibiotics and gave me some oral antibiotics to give him and basically sent him home with me to die stating that he did all that he could.This was a very tough beginning to our Chausie program.

We brought Mongo home and placed him in a small box next to the bed wondering if we were going to see our future chausie sire alive in the morning. I tried to stay up with him most of the night. I kept looking down to see if he were still breathing. It had been a long taxing day and I fell asleep at about 4 am. I awoke with a start at 7 am and quickly remembered the previous day's dilemma. I quickly looked down into the box he had been lying in and he was not there. I figured he had gone off into a corner to die when all of the sudden I heard this banging around only to find him wrestling with Peepers our future chausie queen!!

The veterinarian called in the morning to check on our Jungle Cat Mongo and could not believe that he was still alive!!!!!!

Although the vet was very pleased, he assured me we were not out of the woods yetand that we need to keep a close eye on him. We made repeated trips to the vet and kept him on antibiotics. The diarrhea had subsided and his lung fields slowly began to clear with each visit and follow up x-ray. The vet bills kept mounting but as long as Mongo continued to improve that was fine with us. After three months we were told that all that could be done was done and that only a small portion of his lower lobes still showed problems. We were told that maybe this was some residual scar tissue and he would be fine with it. If not, they would have to do surgery later on and remove the lower lobes.

Mongo's health continued to improve from that day forward and he never did have a relapse. During his recovery process I continued to try to socialize him. He didn't want much to do with humans but would play with cat toys. I would play with him until he was almost exhausted and then while he lay there too tired to fight, I would pet him. One day while petting him, he finally relaxed and started enjoying it!

Mongo is now over two years old and along with Peepers has sired some beautful, huge chausie cubs. We have kept back three of their offspring to use for our second generation chausies (f2's). Mongo is now well over 30 lbs and still putting on weight. His temperament has constantly improved with a lot of patience and handling. He spends many nights in the house and still enjoys sleeping at the foot of our bed. He has developed into a premier Jungle Cat and has been used for commercial modeling pictures. Peepers is a sweet natured queen and proved to be anything but a disappointment. She and Mongo were raised together and they now have kittens in homes in about ten different states. Their chausie kittens are highly sought after due to their size and temperament.

Author's note: The above story was written a couple of years ago. Mongo is now over four years old and Peepers was retired after four litters. She did a fine job.

Jean Cougar, Cleo Panther and PJ Puma are all out of Mongo and Peepers. They are all sisters but not littermates. I picked the biggest and prettiest females out of each of her litters and kept them. Peepers and Mongo did not know how to throw small cubs!

Chapter Eighteen

The Chausie:
Becoming a
Recognized Breed

contributed by
Meryl Peek of
"ReedCat Chausies

Beautiful F2 and F3
Chausie Kittens
from
ReedCat Chausies.

IF ANGELS
TOOK ON THE
BODY OF A CAT...
THE CAT
WOULD NOT ACT
DIFFERENTLY

Chapter Eighteen

The Chausie: Becoming a Recognized Breed

The Jungle Cat hybrid caught the fancy of a breeder, who first applied to The International Cat Association (TICA) for registration status in 1995. Up until then, the Jungle Cat hybrids were referred to as Nile Cats. The Chausie was first granted registration status with TICA in March of 1995 for the purpose of pedigree tracking and establishing a new breed of domestic cat. Chausies continued to be registered with TICA over the following five years, but without any organized group of breeders pursuing the requirements for advancement of the Chausie within TICA.

When the Chausie caught the eye of California breeder, Meryl Peek, of ReedCat Cattery, she tracked down the originator of the breed to see what was being done to advance the Chausie as a show cat in TICA. She directed Meryl to a breeder in Florisa and from that telephone conversation, the two organized an effort to take the breed on through the process of new breed development and recogition. After asking the help of a TICA judge, the *Chausie Breed Standard* was revised to better describe what the breed should look like. It wasn't long before more interested breeders joined into work on breeding programs to develop thebreed toward *Championship Cat* status.

In February 2001, at the Semi-Annual TICA Show and Board Meeting, the Chausie Breed Group asked for and was granted another very exciting step toward becoming a recognized breed and that was *Evaluation Status*. Chausies were, for the first time, permitted into the show hall to be seen and evaluated by licensed TICA judges. This period of time allowed breeders and judges to confer on the breed's goals and development progress and for the judges to become familiar with the Chausie starting at F3 generation. Judges made their reports to the TICA executive office as to whether they thought the Chausie had potential as a distinctive new breed of cat and so far the reports have been favorable.

In next step, the Chausie will advance into *New Breed' Status*. This step will probably take from two to five years. Breeders will be working on looks—until there is consistency of type, fertility in the male Chausies and a wide enough genepool to sustain the Chausie Cat as a breed unique from any other. Imagine, from Jungle Cat hybrid to a Jungle Cat look-a-like that competes internationally along side the pure-bred cats of the world that we are all so familiar with.

Being accepted into the show halls opened another exciting door for the Chausie in 2001. They were accepted for advertising in domestic cat magazines such as Cat Fancy magazine and CATS USA. Chausies also have been given credit in *The New Encyclopedia of the Cat* by Dr. Bruce Fogle, DVM on pages 182-3 featuring REEDCAT'S F1 foundation female, Gazelle. *The New Encyclopedia of the Cat* book is published by DK Publishing, Inc. You can visit their web site at www.dk.com to view their catalogue or order the book.

Chausie breeders have several years ahead of them before the cat is accepted as a *Championship Breed.* Until then they will study the Jungle Cat and its early generation hybrids, always trying to keep this image in the forefront. The goal is to make the Chausie look as much like a Jungle Cat as possible.

WHAT IT TAKES TO MAKE THE CHAMPION CHAUSIE....

The goal of the Chausie breeding program is to retain and mimic the look of the Jungle Cat through selective breeding and preservation of the Jungle Cat's unique features giving the Chausie the visual similarities to that of the Jungle Cat. As breeders breed down the generations, from F1 (first cross) F2, F3, F4 and beyond, the goal is to achieve Championship status (SBT) in TICA making it allowable for the Chausie to compete Internationally with all recognized breeds of pedigreed domestic cats. At Championship level Chausies will be required to have no wild cats within a three-generation pedigree while retaining a visual similarity to its Jungle Cat ancestor preserving such features as large mobile, tufted ears, long legs and a naturally short tail, of three-quarter length, which is about twice the length of a Bobcat's tail and is inherited from the Jungle Cat himself. Full-length tails are also an acceptable length in the Chausie. The Chausie's temperament should be amenable to handling and should exhibit a domestic temperament despite its wild heritage. They are highly intelligent, actively entertaining and are a strikingly exotic cat.

COLORS AND COAT PATTERN OF THE CHAUSIE

The Chausie comes in three colors which mimic the naturally occurring colors and wild ticked coat pattern of the Jungle Cat. The goal is for the Chausie to retain the natural look of the Jungle Cat by allowing only these three colors. Brown Ticked Tabby, Black and Black Silver-Tip. Browns range in shade from a sandy-gray to golden brown through to a reddish-gold to brown coloring. The upper front legs are banded in beautiful black barring and some pattern can also be found on hindlegs and tail. Except for the markings on the legs and tail, the Chausie's coat should be of a ticked pattern only. Although faint spots or stripes are permissible, the preferred coat should closely resemble the ticked coat of the Jungle Cat. Although there is no scientific proof that melanistic Jungle Cats occur, the Chausie has included Solid Black as one of their acceptable color in addition to the Black Silver Tipped color. The Black Silver-Tip is a new color unknown to the domestic cat color genetics. It is unique to the Jungle Cat and is still under study and observation by breeders and TICA geneticists to see how it can be preserved and bred for. Its appearance is one of a black coated cat with silver tipping and banding on the hair shafts. This genetically wild color is also similar to the coat of the Silver Fox. The ticked coat pattern is similar in appearance to a wild hare.

Next time you have a TICA cat show in your area, stop in, you may have the opportunity to see a new breed in the making. A breed that will mimic the look of the Jungle Cat and the first generation hybrids of the same. A breed that is uniquely called a CHAUSIE!!

THANK YOU!!!
FOR PURCHASING
OUR BOOK

Be Sure to Check Out the Newly Released Novel "The Jade Claw" An action/thriller about a man and his beloved Jungle Cat.

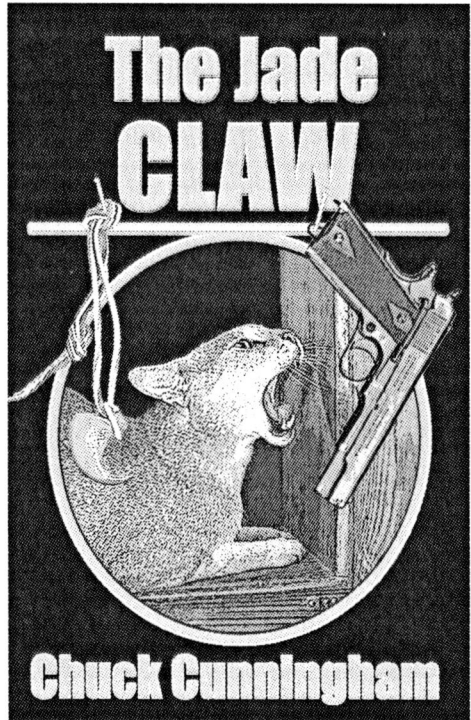

The Jade CLAW

Chuck Cunningham

E-mail comments to:
comments@BlackPantherPublishing.com
Visit our website at: BlackPantherPublishing.com

Printed in the United States
17799LVS00005B/224

9 780972 108218